THIS BOOK BELONGS TO:

LAUNDRY

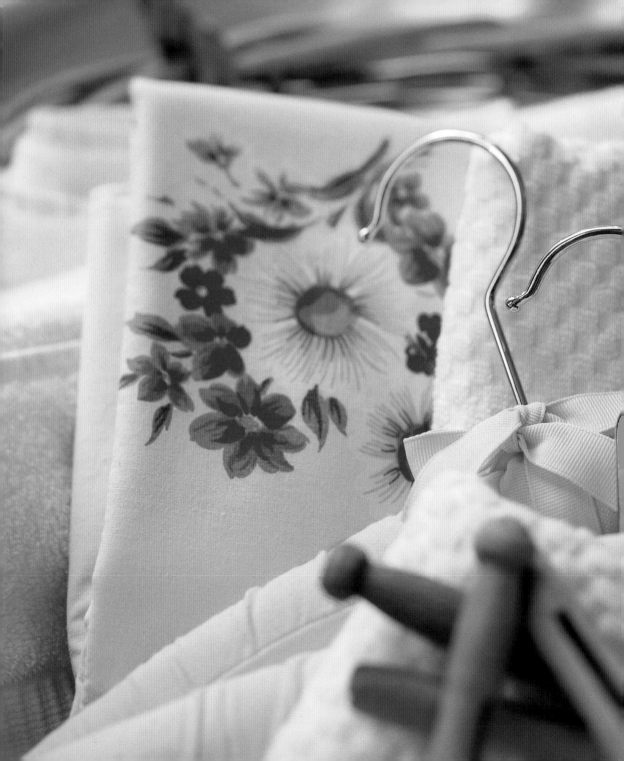

LAUNDRY

THE SPIRIT OF KEEPING HOME

by MONICA NASSIF :: photographs by PATRICK FOX

CHRONICLE BOOKS

SAN FRANCISCO

ACKNOWLEDGMENTS

There are many people to thank when you complete a body of work. First, thanks to the talented people who worked long hours to complete this project swiftly and beautifully: Patrick Fox, photographer; Lisa Evidon, photo stylist; Heidi Madsen, photo stylist assistant; Robyn Warmbo and Darcy Shields Weinstine, book designers and art directors; Ellen Shaffer, whose finesse of language is exquisite; and Mikyla Bruder, our Chronicle Books editor, for her vision and editorial wisdom. Second, to my mother who adored and excelled at laundry in our crazy childhood home of nine children and many pets. She made the mundane task of laundry marvelous, as it offered her solitude, beauty, and tangible evidence of a job well done. And thanks to Mary Dearing, my business partner, who believed in the Caldrea concept when it was a tiny gem of an idea and made it a reality. Amazing, lovely work—thank you.

Library of Congress Cataloging-in-Publication Data available.

ISBN: 0-8118-3984-2

Manufactured in China

Styled by **Lisa Evidon**

Designed by **Warmbo Design**

Distributed in Canada by Raincoast Books

9050 Shaughnessy Street

Vancouver, British Columbia V6P 6E5

10 9 8 7 6 5 4 3 2 1

Chronicle Books LLC

85 Second Street

San Francisco, California 94105

www.chroniclebooks.com

CONTENTS

Joy's soul lies in the doing.
— WILLIAM SHAKESPEARE

INTRODUCTION

In your great-grandmother's day, the fibers were natural, the soaps were simple, and the clothes dryer was a line stretched across the backyard. Today we wear and use enough different fabrics to fill the periodic table of elements. A plethora of presoaks and softeners takes up a whole aisle in the supermarket. And neighborhood associations are getting increasingly touchy about the effect of laundry lines on the landscape.

Fortunately, none of these challenges are insurmountable. In this book, we'll tell you how to stock your laundry room and outline a plan for scheduling, sorting, fluffing, folding, and sending everyone out the door looking great, smelling fresh, and feeling comfortable.

Clean clothing and linens are a delight to the senses. Clean fabrics feel better against the skin. They make the bed—or the body—look cared for and attractive. And, of course, they smell good. The sense of smell is said to be the strongest of our senses and the one with the best memory. The shortest way to our hearts could just as easily be through the laundry room as the kitchen.

In recent years, scientists have started to confirm what herbalists have known for years: that lavender is calming, citruses are uplifting, and patchouli inspires a sense of contentment. But you don't have to be a practicing herbalist—or a degreed chemist—to experience the pleasure that comes from pulling a freshly laundered T-shirt over your head or sliding between clean sheets at the end of a long day.

The process of keeping your clothing and linens clean can be just as fulfilling as the pleasures of wearing and using them. According to the Lotus Sutra, a fundamental text on the teachings of Buddha, clothing and bedding are among the four genuine gifts one human being can give another. (Food and medicine are the other two.)

Every load of laundry starts with a choice. You can make it a chore, approaching it with dread, performing it grudgingly. Or you can choose to take pleasure in the act of caring for yourself and your family. This book, of course, endorses the latter.

Home care as self care is the absolute opposite of that oppressive standard of perfection that makes you feel as though you can never do enough. Please give yourself permission to be human, especially when you're busy and stressed. Let the laundry go for as long as your supply of socks permits. There will always be time later to get caught up.

1

THE RIGHT PLACE & THE RIGHT TIME

How to furnish a well-equipped laundry room and schedule laundry to fit into the life of your home.

LAUNDRY BEGINS LONG BEFORE YOU START YOUR MACHINE.

Where and when you do your laundry can have an enormous impact on how well the job is done—and how much you enjoy it. Giving yourself the gift of a pleasant place to work is the first step in transforming the task of laundry from an onerous chore to a rewarding ritual. And giving yourself the gift of sufficient time is the next step.

1. THE LAUNDRY ROOM

In so many homes, the laundry room is an afterthought. The machines are stashed in a busy back hallway or a dark, damp basement, shoved up against a grungy utility sink. Maybe there's a shelf for detergents. Maybe there's a dilapidated table for folding or no room for folding at all. And maybe there's a reason why you don't like doing the laundry.

You probably don't have to go to great lengths, like hiring a contractor to add a state-of-the-art laundry wing to your house—or moving—to create a space that's more conducive to laundry. It's quite possible to achieve a brighter, better laundry room with minimal expenditures of time and effort. Consider the following features and decide which ones will help your laundry room serve you better.

Light Natural light is ideal, but even a windowless room can be brightly lit to help you see stains before they're set. Supplement your standard-issue overhead light with one or two lamps that will accommodate lightbulbs of at least 75 watts. Adjustable reading lamps, either tabletop versions or floor models, can be easily positioned to help you see the black sock left behind in the washer before it turns your next load of white towels gray.

Work surface Give yourself as much space for sorting and folding as the size of your room and the state of your budget will allow. Washable, nonporous surfaces are best, since this area will be subject to occasional spills and dribbles from laundry products. If you have room for a table, affordable vintage variations range from rustic farmhouse antiques to funky 1950s chrome-and-laminate models. If your laundry is located in a well-traveled back hallway, ask a handyman to help you install a countertop on hinges that can fold flat against the wall when not in use.

Cabinets, cupboards, and shelves Between detergents, softeners, additives, and stain removers, it's ridiculously easy to amass a dozen bottles, boxes, and canisters in your laundry. Open shelves, while convenient, can easily turn into clutter. Inexpensive kitchen-style cabinetry can be a great storage solution. A freestanding cupboard, like an antique pie safe, also will do the job nicely.

Hanging space A rolling garment rack or a small, well-ventilated closet gives you a place to hang garments fresh from the dryer to help keep wrinkles at bay. You can even get a small tension rod from a hardware store and install it in a doorway if you don't have enough room for something more permanent. If money is no object, invest in some good wooden hangers. If money is an object, inexpensive plastic hangers are kinder to your clothes than wire ones.

Humidity control If your laundry is located in the basement, and you live in a climate where high humidity is a reliably regular weather factor, invest in a dehumidifier. This will keep the air smelling fresher, protect your laundry from mildew, and ensure that your drip-dry underthings will be ready to wear in the morning.

Ironing supplies If space permits, the laundry room is the handiest place in the house to keep your ironing board, iron, linen sprays, and starch. If you can touch up trousers fresh from the dryer and press linen napkins as soon as the washer stops spinning, you will be far less likely to find yourself with a backlog of ironing projects.

Music Because laundry seldom demands your full attention and concentration, the laundry room is the perfect place to enjoy music that underscores the natural rhythms of sorting and folding. Put on some Nina Simone or Ella Fitzgerald. Sing along.

2. THE HOUSEHOLD LAUNDRY SCHEDULE

Plenty of people—intelligent people with responsible jobs—do laundry according to the Brink of Doom system. The fundamental assumption of this system is that the best day to do your laundry is the day before you run out of shirts, socks, or unmentionables. At first glance, this seems like a sensible plan. But exactly how much mental energy do you spend keeping a running tally of available socks? How do you synchronize the emptying of your sock drawer with the emptying of your underwear drawer? Even assuming that you can tally and synchronize with the best of them, how on earth can you manage to do this for more than one person at a time?

If you have ever used the Brink of Doom laundry system, you have almost certainly suffered at least one of the consequences of system failure: a morning without clean socks or (worse) a morning without clean underwear. Mornings are difficult enough without a calamity of this magnitude. Should this happen to you, resist the temptation to blame yourself. Blame the system. It only takes one brief distraction or one tiny miscalculation and, the next thing you know, you're waking up to a very disagreeable day.

There is only one known solution to the Brink of Doom. In your grandmother's day it used to be called Wash Day. Two generations ago, Wash Day happened once a week. It started first thing in the morning, and it lasted until everything washable was washed, dried, folded, and put away. Today you get to define the parameters of Wash Day. You even get to decide what you want to call it.

Maybe Sundays work best for your household, so that everyone starts the week with everything they need. If the prospect of laundry casts a long, bleak shadow across your treasured weekends, maybe you'd prefer to schedule it for the two or three weeknights when you're not driving yourself or your children to piano lessons, basketball practice, or committee meetings. Maybe you'll assign towels to one day, sheets to another, and clothing to a third.

The actual structure of your laundry schedule can be whatever suits you and the needs of your household. The important thing is to create a schedule you can stick to—and then stick to it. This is especially important if you're enlisting your child, spouse, or roommate to help you with the laundry. It's hard for anyone to commit to a moving target. Set a fixed time each week.

To create the best laundry schedule for you, start with a working knowledge of how often each item needs washing. Adapt the following guidelines to your household and your standards for acceptable cleanliness.

TECHNIQUE | LAUNDERING FREQUENCY

SHEETS	Once a week, or more frequently, if someone is ill
BLANKETS	Once a month
BATH TOWELS	Same schedule as sheets; launder more frequently in hot, humid weather
KITCHEN TOWELS	For people with busy kitchens (lots of cooking from scratch or children) change daily; for those who live alone and eat out frequently, a weekly schedule
SHIRTS, PANTS, SHORTS, & SKIRTS	After each wearing or after every second wearing, if there are no noticeable traces of perspiration or stains
UNMENTIONABLES	After each wearing for briefs and panties; bras after every second wearing, if they pass the sniff test
SOCKS & WORKOUT GEAR	After each wearing

2

A GOOD START

1. **STAIN REMOVAL**

2. **SORTING**

How to remedy spots and spills, sort your laundry into compatible loads, and attend to oft-overlooked details such as pocket stowaways and unzipped zippers.

PATIENT ATTENTION TO DETAIL IS ITS OWN REWARD.

To prepare your laundry for the wash is to take pleasure in every aspect of the job well done.

Nevertheless, when time is tight, it can be very tempting to heave an armload of laundry into the washer and hope for the best. But the time you save by skipping stain removal won't seem like such a bargain when you discover a permanent spot on your favorite shirt. And the ten seconds it takes to take a tissue out of a pocket is time well spent compared to the ten minutes you'd otherwise spend removing a veritable blizzard of lint from a week's worth of work clothes.

You'll always get far better results by investing a few minutes to treat stains, empty pockets, zip zippers, and sort your laundry into compatible wash loads. But try not to succumb to perfectionism. Even the most conscientious of us will overlook the occasional sauce spot or fail to catch a pocketed pen. When this happens to you, don't be too hard on yourself. Just take a deep breath, figure out what you can do to minimize the damage, and remember—it's just stuff.

1. STAIN REMOVAL

The science of stain removal is far from foolproof. Stains are complicated chemistry: You need to consider both the characteristics of the fiber and the ingredients of the stain itself. A technique that works like a charm on sturdy cotton may shred a delicate silk.

A single plan of attack is usually sufficient for simple stains like juice or mud. But cosmetic and sauce stains are twice as challenging because they have two different components: oils, which leave grease stains, and pigments, which compound your problem by leaving colorful traces of lipstick or tomatoes behind.

Although there are no guarantees when it comes to stain removal, the best thing you can do to improve your chances is to act as quickly as possible. Stains that are still wet are less likely to set than stains that have been allowed to dry. A one-day-old stain is easier to deal with than one that has been left untreated for a week.

FIRST AID

Before you apply anything to a stain, try to remove as much of the staining substance as possible without spreading it. For liquids, like wine or blood, blot the stain with a clean, white towel or napkin. Resist the urge to rub—you'll just grind the stain into the fibers. For thicker substances, like sauces or mud, scrape away as much as you can with a smooth-bladed table knife. Never use a sharp chef's knife or a serrated blade; it could cut the threads or damage the fabric.

A laundry professional who does thirty-five loads a day for a large estate uses an embroidery hoop to stretch a stained fabric taut. Then she positions the stain under a magnifying glass and prods the stain with a needle, thread by thread, until it comes out.

NEXT STEPS

If the item is washable, try dabbing it with a little club soda or cool water (never hot water), then blot again. Then try the remedies suggested here. Always wash the item after treating but check the stain before you put it into the dryer. If it isn't gone, treat it again. It may take several tries to remove a stain completely. A stain that has been set by the heat of the dryer will probably be with you for the life of the garment.

If the item is dry-clean only, simply take it to the cleaners as soon as possible—water or club soda may damage the fabric and impede your cleaner's ability to remove the stain.

THE POWER OF PLAIN WATER

Fresh coffee, fruit, and tea stains will often come out with clear water. Simply stretch the stained fabric across the top of a large, ceramic bowl and secure it with an elastic band or an embroidery hoop to keep it taut. Place this arrangement in your bathtub. Then, standing outside the tub, pour water (boiling is best if the fabric can tolerate high temperatures) from a height of about three feet. Go slowly at first, taking care not to splash or burn yourself.

TIP | SUPPLIES FOR STAIN REMOVAL

If you prefer to avoid harsh chemicals like chlorine bleach and most commercial stain removers, stock your laundry room with the following items to help you tackle most stains on washable fabrics.

Borax powder (available in the laundry aisle)

Clear dish soap

Complexion brush or soft toothbrush for gentle scrubbing

Cornstarch or talcum powder (to absorb grease)

Cotton swabs and cotton balls, for dabbing remedies on stains

Enzyme presoak products

Eyedroppers, to flush small stains

Hair spray (the old-fashioned kind with no extras)

Isopropyl (rubbing) alcohol

Glycerin (available at drugstores)

Lemon juice (may bleach dark fabrics)

Salt

White vinegar

STAIN REMEDIES FOR WASHABLE FABRICS

We wish we could guarantee these methods, but stains are often wilier than we are. Proceed with caution. And trust your own judgment—if you suspect that a remedy may be too harsh or damaging, consult an expert. On the other hand, if the stain has rendered the item unusable or unwearable anyway, you may have nothing to lose by trying an extreme measure.

STAIN	REMEDY
BLOOD	Rinse well in cold water or soak in cold salt water. Wash in cold water.
CHOCOLATE	Wet the stain and sprinkle with dry borax. Scrub gently with a toothbrush. Use an enzyme presoak. Soak the stain in club soda. Follow all remedies with a cold-water wash.
COFFEE	Apply vinegar.
EGG	Soak in cold salt water. Follow with a cold-water wash.
FRUIT & VEGETABLE JUICES	Wet fabric and sprinkle with salt. Then rinse and apply dish soap. Apply isopropyl alcohol. Then rinse and apply white vinegar.
GRASS	Apply isopropyl alcohol. Rinse and apply dish soap.
GUM	Put item in the freezer or apply ice until gum is brittle enough to scrape off. Soak any remaining residue in vinegar.
INK	Apply glycerin and rub well. Let stand at least fifteen minutes then apply dish soap and water. For felt-tip ink, apply isopropyl alcohol.
MAKEUP	Spritz with hair spray. Flush with vinegar.
MUD	Scrape off as much as possible. Soak in warm water and laundry detergent then launder as usual.
MUSTARD	Apply dish soap.

Some remedies—particularly lemon juice—may fade or bleach colored fabrics. Test these remedies on an inconspicuous corner or inner seam first. Some stains have more than one remedy. Never apply two remedies at once! Certain chemical combinations, notably vinegar and baking soda, can have explosive consequences. Always rinse the item thoroughly, or launder it, before trying another approach.

STAIN	REMEDY
OILY SAUCES OR SALAD DRESSINGS	Rub stain with dry talc or cornstarch to absorb as much grease as possible. Work powder into the fabric with a toothbrush. Then apply laundry detergent generously and wash in the warmest water the care label allows.
RUST	Apply lemon juice.
SAUCES & CONDIMENTS	Apply vinegar.
SOY SAUCE	Wet fabric and apply dish soap.
TEA	Apply lemon juice then rinse and launder as usual.
WAX	Put item in the freezer or apply ice until wax is brittle enough to scrape off. If residue remains, place fabric between two clean rags and apply a warm iron. If the mark is still visible, apply a few drops of vegetable oil and work gently into the stain. Let sit for fifteen minutes then blot as much of the oil as you can with paper towels. Rub with talc or cornstarch (to absorb remaining oil). Dab generously with laundry detergent and wash in the warmest water the care label allows.
WINE, RED	Apply isopropyl alcohol. Apply vinegar. Apply salt to absorb as much as possible; then flush the stain with vodka and wash immediately.
WINE, WHITE	Rinse well with water then launder as usual.

If the stained item is irreplaceable, please consider putting it into the hands of a professional, even if the fabric is washable. Their arsenal of skills and cleaning solutions is almost certainly more complete than yours. And, unlike you, they're not emotionally involved. The stress of returning a priceless textile or a treasured, handmade gift to its original, pristine state has been known to wilt even the most experienced, well-equipped amateur.

2. SORTING

Many of the very same people who do laundry according to the Brink of Doom system—the intelligent ones with the responsible jobs—also fail to sort their laundry before washing it. Perhaps sorting laundry seems like a waste of time to them. Or maybe it seems like a waste of water to wash fewer than the absolute maximum number of articles that can be crammed into the machine.

Nonsorters are easy to spot. Their whites are tinged with gray. Their knits are stretched or shrunken. The collars of their shirts are curled and their plackets are puckered. They return a lot more clothes to the store than sorters do, and complain a lot more about how standards of quality have declined precipitously. None of which seems worth the two or three minutes a week they save by not sorting their laundry.

If you think those two or three minutes a week might be wisely applied toward avoiding unnecessary trips to the store and achieving a relatively smooth, crumple-free appearance, then sorting is for you.

Sorting is a good idea for several reasons. All fabrics are not created equal. Some require hot water and vigorous agitation. Others need gentle soap and tepid temperatures. And many are colored by dyes that will fade if laundered at the wrong temperature or bleed onto more impressionable items if they rumble with the wrong crowd.

The sorting process also provides you with an opportunity to attend to little details that prevent not-so-little laundry mishaps. Zip zippers, close Velcro closures, and snap snaps to keep them from catching on other fabrics. Turn velveteen fabrics and corduroys inside out to keep the pile from matting. And turn knits inside out to protect them from snagging.

Deciding where to sort your laundry is a matter of personal preference and practicality. If you have the space, install a big table or countertop in your laundry room. If you're living in tight quarters, a collection of small, nesting laundry baskets will do the job nicely. You can even sort laundry in piles on the floor. (Though this depends on the floor. The floor of your bedroom is probably fine. The floor of your apartment building's communal laundry area is almost certainly not.)

In addition to being convenient and clean, your sorting space also needs to be well lighted. Good lighting makes it much easier to read teeny little care labels (more on those in a minute) and spot teeny little stains. Once you've decided on a place that works for you, simply create as many piles as you need.

Delicates Pile all your delicate cycle items together. These are the things with tags that say, "Machine wash gentle cycle" or "Machine wash cold." Then sort these by color into two or three wash loads: light and dark, or light, medium, and dark.

Whites Pile all your white clothing together. (Decide whether you'll allow ecru, oyster, and other near-whites. If not, make another pile.)

Towels and sheets Sort these separately from other laundry of similar colors; you can usually use hotter water than if you mix these items with garments in the same load.

Darks Pile all your dark things together.

Jeans Keep jeans separate from other dark clothing.

Brights Pile brightly colored items together.

Mediums Pile all the things that aren't white, bright, dark, or delicate (otherwise known as the "mediums") together. This includes gray sweats, neutral polo shirts, khaki pants, and so on.

New items Bright and dark items that haven't been washed before should be segregated from other wash loads.

After a week of particularly muddy gardening, exceedingly rugged camping, or extravagantly messy baking, it's a good idea to create a special pile for items that are heavily soiled and therefore good candidates for a presoaking or an extra-long wash cycle. Do this load as soon as possible to keep soils from becoming stains.

Once you've organized your laundry into compatible groups, one final step remains: assembling well-balanced wash loads. A well-balanced wash load contains a balance of small, medium, and large items. Wet fabrics are much heavier than dry ones, and their weight can shift as the machine agitates and spins. A wash load full of heavy towels, jeans, and blankets will often throw the machine out of balance, creating ghastly clunking noises and bringing the cycle to a halt. You'll then have to redistribute the laundry in the drum before the machine can complete the cycle.

Unbalanced loads happen to everyone occasionally. If they happen regularly, however, the extra wear and tear will prematurely age your washer. So will cramming too many clothes into each load. Load your laundry without pushing or compressing it and stop when the machine is almost full. There needs to be enough room for water to circulate freely among your items. Overfilling the machine will compromise its cleaning power and expose your fabrics to excessive friction that will make them old before their time. And it will put you on a first name basis with the guys who make house calls to fix washers, tsk-tsking all the while because nobody knows how to do laundry properly anymore.

To sort laundry successfully, it's important to read the care labels sewn into each item. If you've never done this before, don't be distressed by the prospect of adding additional minutes to your routine. The human memory is a marvelous thing, and as you grow accustomed to sorting your laundry week after week, you will soon know at a glance where to allocate each item. Please see page 41 for a guide to the mysterious triangles, squiggles, and other symbols that appear on care labels.

TIP | POCKET STOWAWAYS

While you're sorting, be sure to empty pockets. Be ruthless and thorough. A single missed tissue will turn your dryer into a lint festival. Pocket change will cause premature aging in both your clothes and your washer. Golf tees will snag delicate knits. Undetected lipsticks and pens can permanently ruin an entire wash load—and the effects may linger to mar subsequent loads as well. Even if a pocket's contents aren't a hazard to the wash load, the washer can be a hazard to the contents—after twenty-five minutes of agitation and spinning, your favorite reading glasses could be warped beyond repair.

3

WATER & AIR

1. WASHING

2. DRYING

Getting to know your machines and their cycles, using detergents and softeners, deciphering fabric care labels, washing new clothes, washing by hand, and machine drying vs. line drying.

ONCE YOUR LAUNDRY IS LOADED INTO THE MACHINE,

you have almost an hour to call your own. This time is utterly guilt-free—after all, you're still accomplishing something. So resist the temptation to multitask, and use the time wisely to take care of yourself.

You can brew a cup of tea. Curl up with a book. Pick up your knitting. Call an old friend. Laundry is a wonderful excuse to stay in and enjoy all the cozy comforts of home.

1. WASHING

ALL ABOUT WASHERS

Even though the engineering of washing machines has been dramatically refined in the last decade, most consumers still do laundry the way their mothers taught them. Manufacturers have lavished their newest machines with all kinds of interactive gadgetry designed to coddle luxury fibers, wrestle jeans into submission, and target stains with laserlike precision. To the consumer, all of these innovations can seem even more time-consuming than Mom's methods. It can take up to fifteen hours a week to do the laundry for a household with children. So when, exactly, are you supposed to find the time to run the fragile silk nightie cycle?

Of course, technology has been making impressive strides in solving laundry problems ever since the day the washboard was officially rendered obsolete. But until someone invents a microwave washer that can do a load of towels in the time it takes to thaw a frozen burrito, laundry remains one of the most time-consuming tasks in the home. So it makes sense to give the tasks of selecting and maintaining a washer as much time and attention as you can spare.

All washers are different—especially the newer ones. Your owner's manual may not be fascinating reading, but it will save you time over the long run if you take a few minutes to learn how to make the most of your new machine.

Top-loading vs. front-loading Most American-made washing machines are top-loading models, and most commercially available laundry products are formulated exclusively for these machines. Top-loading washers are easier to load and unload because you don't have to bend over to reach into the drum. And they are usually larger in capacity to accommodate the big loads of laundry Americans prefer.

Front-loading machine

Top-loading machine

Front-loading machines are new to the American market but have long been the norm in Europe, where strict conservation standards and minuscule apartments require smaller, more efficient machines. These machines use about half as much water as American top-loading models. Their cycle times tend to be longer than top-loading machines.

Instead of agitating like top-loading models, the motion of front-loading washers is similar to a dryer; the laundry is cleaned as the drum rotates. In these machines, conventional laundry detergents produce an excess of suds. In areas where there are few low-suds detergent formulas available to consumers, use half the recommended amount of product in front-loading machines.

Cleaning and sanitizing   It may seem odd to consider cleaning a machine that receives regular inundations of detergent and water, but there are some occasions when these extra steps are a good idea. Most washing machines have lint traps that can clog over time, reducing their efficiency. If you can't figure out where yours is, check your owner's manual. Then clean it once a month or so.

Soaps, lint, and minerals from the water will leave deposits in your washer, especially if you live in an area with hard water. Over time, this residue can diminish your washer's performance and leave deposits on your fabrics. Once a year, add a quart of white vinegar to a full-size, hot water wash to dissolve any buildup. (Do not wash any laundry in this cycle.) Follow with a rinse cycle of clear water.

Back in the days when most wash loads were hardy enough for hot water and chlorine bleach, only the most finicky homemakers would have considered sanitizing their washing machines. But now that most loads are done in warm or cold water, and bleach is used more sparingly, your washer may be harboring something more sinister than the occasional stray sock. You can sanitize your machine on a quarterly basis, as a precautionary measure, or on a situational basis, depending on the special needs of your household.

TECHNIQUE | THREE REASONS TO SANITIZE YOUR WASHER

1. You have just moved into a home with a washer used by a previous occupant.

2. Your household is fighting a cold or flu bug.

3. You are washing baby diapers at home.

To sanitize a washer tub, add a cup of oxygen bleach to a full-size, hot water wash cycle. (Do not add laundry to this cycle.) Allow the water to drain, then run a rinse cycle of clear water.

DETERGENTS AND SOFTENERS

Detergents were developed as alternatives to old-fashioned alkaline soaps because soaps do not dissolve well in hard water. (Which is why you get that recurring soap scum ring in your bathtub—but that's another book.) Today's all-purpose laundry powders are designed to work in hot, warm, or cold water. Many contain oxygen bleach to fight stains and odors. The most effective laundry detergents are formulated to rinse away completely, leaving no residue to stiffen fabrics or irritate skin. Read the labels and follow your nose; the smell of your detergent will be your daily companion so it makes sense to find a fragrance you will enjoy.

Detergents designed for delicate items are especially formulated for the gentle cycle and hand washing delicates in the bathroom sink. These products clean gently, and effectively, without bleaching.

For best results, add detergent as the washer is filling with water. Wait to add your laundry until the water level is about half to three-quarters full. Detergent added after the laundry is loaded won't dissolve and distribute itself as evenly through the wash water, and may leave faded spots on fabrics.

Liquid fabric softener is added during the final rinse to help fabrics feel better, smell better, and resist static. Use it sparingly, according to the package directions, to prevent buildup. Many people choose to exclude softeners when washing towels; they can make cottons somewhat less absorbent.

THE DIFFERENCE BETWEEN HARD AND SOFT WATER

Two naturally occurring minerals, calcium and magnesium, determine whether your water is hard or soft. Hard water contains as much as ten times more of these minerals than soft water. More than 85 percent of all water in the United States is hard.

Hard water inhibits soaps from lathering well and rinsing completely, resulting in residues that linger on laundry, skin, hair, and hard surfaces, such as tubs and sinks. Home water softeners use salts to counteract the effects of hard water minerals. Although these salts will improve the performance of your soaps and shampoos, chemically softened water should not be used as drinking water.

TECHNIQUE | TWO SECRETS TO WHITER WHITES

1. Wrap the peel of one lemon in cheese-cloth or muslin and tie securely closed. Add to the wash cycle.

2. Dilute a quarter cup of hydrogen peroxide with a cup of water; add at the beginning of the rinse cycle.

120°F / 49°C

105°F / 41°C

85°F / 29°C

Hot water washing Generations ago, hot water was the standard. But few of today's fabric care labels recommend hot water, generally defined as temperatures of 120°F or above. For fibers that can take the heat, hot water is the most effective for removing stains, eliminating soil, and killing germs and dust mites. Whites and colorfast items—such as diapers, gym socks, many sheets, and most towels—are the best candidates for hot water washing. Hot water will cause many dark dyes to fade over time.

Warm water washing According to fabric care labels, the ideal warm water wash is achieved at a temperature of approximately 105°F. This temperature is recommended for many blends and synthetics, as well as some non-colorfast fabrics. Warm water washing is sufficient for removing most light-to-moderate soil and many stains, especially if pretreated beforehand. Bright and medium-colored items are the best candidates for warm water washing.

Cold water washing Temperatures of 85°F or less are kindest to deep and bright colors, unstable dyes, and delicate fabrics such as silks and woolens. Since cold water is less effective at removing stains, it is important to inspect items carefully and spot treat stains before washing. Be sure to use a detergent especially formulated for cold water loads; not all formulas dissolve completely at cooler temperatures.

If you prefer to wash lingerie items in a cold water delicate cycle, pick up a small mesh laundry bag, available in housewares stores. The bag will keep your underthings from losing their shape prematurely—and protect the rest of your load from being snagged by hooks and hardware.

CYCLE TIMES

Many of the newest washing machines feature specific cycle times for various kinds of wash loads. If your machine doesn't offer such structured advice, a wash cycle of six to eight minutes in a standard, top-loading washer is plenty for the ordinary grime of everyday laundry. Unnecessarily long wash cycles can cause excessive wear and fading. Increase the cycle time for loads that are heavily soiled.

Front-loading washers may require longer cycle times. If your owner's manual doesn't give you the answers you're looking for, check with the manufacturer's Web site or call their customer service number. Because makers of front-loading washers are anxious to see their products achieve greater acceptance in the American market, you will find them eager to help.

WASHING NEW THINGS

It's not absolutely essential to wash newly purchased clothing, bedding, or linens before wearing or using, except for baby things. However it's a good idea, especially if the fabric will come in direct contact with your skin. Manufacturers frequently treat textiles with fabric finishes to help the clothes look their best while they are in the store. These finishes are formulated to resist wrinkles, inhibit crumpling, and protect fabrics from the grime of repeated handling and trying on of garments. They are not necessarily formulated to be kind to sensitive skin. Even garments without such finishes may be harboring traces of dye.

Items with non-colorfast dyes may run and bleed the first few times they are laundered, so it will take several washings before they're fit to share the washing machine with other things. If a care label says, "Wash separately," the item is not colorfast. If the item has no care label at all, dip an inconspicuous corner into a sinkfull of cool water to see whether the dye will run.

In a perfect world, anything with a care label that says, "Wash separately," would always be lovingly washed by hand in the bathroom sink. In the real world, the second-best solution is usually adequate: Machine-wash the item by itself for the first time, in cold water, on a gentle cycle setting. After that, it should be safe to wash the item with laundry of similar or darker colors.

LIQUIDS, POWDERS, AND SOAPS

When it comes to effectiveness, there's truly no difference between liquid and powdered laundry detergents. It's really a matter of personal preference—some people buy powders because they're lighter and easier to carry than comparable amounts of liquid detergents.

Powders tend to be highly concentrated, provided that they don't contain dyes or fillers. You need only a small amount to complete a load of laundry. Powders containing oxygen bleach are especially formulated to clean whites and colors effectively and rinse without a trace.

One of the main ingredients in liquid detergents is water, one of nature's best solvents. For the best value and performance, look for highly concentrated formulations that are free of petrochemicals.

Old-fashioned laundry soap is almost impossible to find in the modern marketplace. Soaps don't rinse as cleanly as detergents, so they can leave residue on your laundry and soapy scum in your washing machine. Occasionally you may find lovely, indulgent French laundry soaps in specialty stores—some people swear by them for delicates and linens. If you find them and want to give them a try, use small amounts for hand laundering only. Rinse several times in cool water to remove any lingering film.

FABRIC CARE LABELS

The Federal Trade Commission introduced this standardized system of symbols in 1997 so that consumers would know precisely how to care for their clothing and linens in any language.

Courtesy of: The Soap and Detergent Association, 1500 K Street, NW, Suite 300, Washington, DC 20005 www.cleaning101.com
Developed in cooperation with the Federal Trade Commission

Hand washing is the method of choice for your delicate, vintage, and valuable items. Washing your delicates by hand takes less than ten minutes. Make it a pleasant part of your nightly ritual, like caring for your complexion and brushing your teeth. For best results, always wash the following items by hand.

1. Fill the basin with cool water. (Ice-cold water is hard on the hands.) Add a capful of delicate wash detergent. (Mild hand soap liquid works in a pinch.)

2. Swish the items, one or two at a time, gently through the suds. Soak for five minutes. Then drain the basin and gently squeeze the sudsy water from your delicates.

3. Rinse twice, each time in a basin full of clean water. Rinse a third time if any soap remains after the second rinse.

Lingerie A single garment usually comprises a variety of materials, each with its own idiosyncratic tendency to shrink or stretch.

Lacy fabrics Fragile lacy fabrics are easily snagged.

Embroidered or highly textured items The embroidery can be damaged by friction.

Non-colorfast textiles The dyes can bleed.

Heirloom pieces Fabrics made before care labels were invented are best washed by hand.

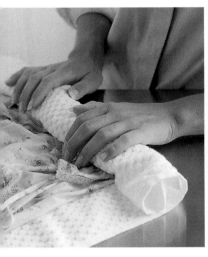  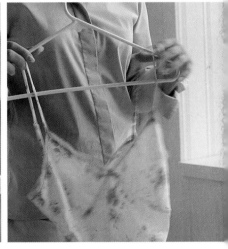

4. Squeeze items gently and roll them in a clean, colorfast towel. (Consider buying some large white towels just for this purpose so you can keep your "good towels" clean and dry.)

5. Press the towel gently to remove as much water as you can without altering the shape or structure of the garment.

6. Hang to dry on a plastic or wooden hanger, a drying rack, an indoor laundry line, or a nonmetallic shower rod. To help sweaters and other knits to maintain their shape, invest in a sweater dryer: a flat, mesh platform on a raised wooden or plastic stand.

WASHING BY HAND: ON THE ROAD

Many hotel bathrooms are equipped with retractable laundry lines for drip-drying hand-washed items. If yours is not, a wooden or plastic hanger hung on the shower rod is a good substitute. Wire hangers are not; they can leave rust marks and stretched-out shoulder bumps on wet garments. Stores that cater to travelers frequently sell inflatable hangers for drying shirts.

Travel-size packages of laundry detergent are hard to come by, so seasoned travelers make a habit of decanting their own. Laundry powder travels well in a small plastic bag with a zip closure. For liquids, use the small plastic or aluminum travel bottles available at discount stores. If you find yourself stranded without detergent, a capful of shampoo will do, as long as it isn't one of those shampoo-with-conditioner formulas or one of the new color fortifying shampoos designed to brighten your highlights.

The towel drying method, described in the previous section about hand washing at home, is especially important if you need your wash to be dry by checkout time. Don't be shy about asking the housekeeping department for an extra towel.

2. DRYING

MACHINE DRYING

Tumble drying is too often regarded as a necessary evil, a distant second best to the bucolic charms of the old-fashioned backyard laundry line. But there are actually several reasons to prefer the humble services of your tumble dryer. Line drying knits will often stretch the fabric, distorting the fit. Terry-cloth towels can look matted and feel stiff when line dried (though some people prefer the rough texture of line-dried towels as an easy exfoliating treatment). If you're an apartment-bound city dweller, drying laundry on an outdoor line is about as doable as raising your own cattle. Even if you live in the country, the weather forecast can render the laundry line unusable for entire weeks—or entire seasons.

Maybe the tumble dryer's second-class status explains why few people pay it as much attention as they do the washing machine. But a thoughtful approach to drying will reward you with piles and piles of fresh, warm, fluffy, static-free laundry.

If your household is battling allergies or a cold or flu bug, high-temperature tumble drying will also help to neutralize dust mites, pollens, and germs (provided that the fabrics are sturdy enough to survive without shrinking or falling apart).

As you transfer your laundry from the washer to the dryer, you will notice that a wash load of wet clothing looks like less than half a load in the dryer. Resist the temptation to fill the dryer drum with two wash loads or more. You won't save any time—in fact, an overload may take more time to dry than two appropriately sized single loads. And differing wash loads with differing colors are actually more likely to bleed in the dryer than in the washing machine.

Dryers are sized to correspond to the size of washing machines. An appropriately sized wash load is also an appropriately sized dryer load. The drying process requires plenty of room for air to circulate, and fabrics will fluff and expand as they dry.

Most newly manufactured dryers are equipped with sensors that monitor the moisture level of the load and shut the machine off when the load is suitably dry. This feature takes the guesswork out of the process and helps protect laundry from overcooking, which can cause premature wear and aggravate static cling.

If your dryer is not equipped with a moisture sensor, you'll need to set the cycle timer. Drying time is usually twice as long as washing time. Since the typical wash cycle is about twenty-five minutes, the typical dryer cycle is about fifty minutes. Allow an extra ten minutes or so for thick, heavy fabrics like towels or jeans. If the load is small, or the fabrics are predominately lightweight, dial the dryer time down to about forty minutes.

Some clothing items, like cotton knits, look best if they are removed a few minutes before they are completely dry. A little bit of dampness, especially in the seams, will make it easier to smooth and straighten the garments so that they don't need to be ironed. If you are using a dryer without a moisture sensor, pay close attention to synthetic loads, which can go from perfectly dry to crackling-with-static in mere minutes.

Check heavy items, like towels and jeans, to make sure they are completely dry before you fold them and put them away, especially in damp or humid weather. Slightly moist fabrics, when stored in enclosed closets or drawers, will not remain fresh smelling for long.

Like washing machines, most dryers offer three temperature choices: high, low (or gentle), and cool (or air fluff).

Use the hot cycle for regular wash loads of sheets, towels, socks, cotton underwear, jeans, and diapers. If the care label says, "Tumble dry," the high cycle is usually safe. If you have any concerns about shrinking, use the low cycle instead.

The low cycle circulates warm air, rather than hot. Use this cycle for synthetics, dryer-safe delicates, and items with care labels that read, "Tumble dry medium" or "Tumble dry low."

The air fluff cycle simply tumbles the contents of the dryer without heat. Use this cycle to revive pillows and comforters or to freshen clean clothes that have been packed for traveling or folded away in storage. This cycle can also be used to hasten the drying time of no-heat items such as plastic shower curtains and elasticized exercise gear.

Softeners in the dryer If you have used liquid fabric softener in the wash cycle, you shouldn't add a softener to the dryer. Over-softened fabrics are like over-conditioned hair: limp and almost greasy. Dryer softening is best suited for synthetics that otherwise develop static cling. If you have sensitive skin, avoid using conventional dryer softeners on garments worn next to the skin. Overuse of dryer sheets will leave a waxy residue on your dryer drum.

If you need to use a softening agent in the dryer but you don't like the strong, synthetic fragrances of dryer sheets, simply dab a small amount of liquid softener on a wet, clean towel or rag and add it to the dryer at the start of the cycle. (Consider buying a few inexpensive white washcloths for this purpose.) Don't use as much as you would in a wash load—your dryer has no rinse cycle to carry away any excess. Start small and adjust until you achieve satisfactory results.

Maintaining your dryer   The most important thing you can do is to clean the lint filter after every load. A clogged lint filter can slow a dryer down dramatically. And excess lint is a serious fire hazard. If your dryer is vented to the outside, detach the duct—either the dryer end or the vent end, whichever is easier—and clear it of lint once a year.

If an undetected staining stowaway, like a pen or a lipstick, has left its mark on a dryer full of clothes, be sure to inspect the dryer drum carefully and remove all traces of the offending substance from every surface and crevice before you load the dryer again. Avoid abrasives— your dryer drum needs to be smooth to avoid snagging fabrics. Simply moisten a soft rag with a small dab of all-purpose cleaning liquid and rub gently. Follow with a clean, wet rag to remove any cleanser residue.

ASIDE | AROMATHERAPY COMES HOME

Aromatherapy is the practice of using the essential oils of plants, flowers, and herbs to enhance psychological and physical well-being. Modern research continues to validate what traditional practitioners have always known about the powers and pleasures of fragrant essential oils—they simply make you feel as good as they smell. Lavender helps you to relax; citrus uplifts and energizes; and patchouli inspires and soothes.

Although these benefits have long been available in a wide range of bath, body, and cosmetic products, only recently have the pleasures of aromatherapy been available for the care of your clothes and linens. Today you can scent your sanctuary to suit your mood—and use the enhancing aspects of aromatherapy to add a sense of enchantment to your laundry day.

LINE DRYING OUTDOORS

The practice of hanging laundry outside to dry has many dedicated fans, for good reasons. It's healthy—sunlight kills germs—and it makes laundry smell good. But the bucolic image of unbleached sheets undulating gently in the summer breeze omits a few details that are considerably less picturesque.

Like birds, for example. Unless you can somehow enforce a no-fly zone over your laundry line, you will quickly learn that birds are just as likely to drop unpleasant remnants of avian digestion on your pillowcases as anywhere. Although you can't completely prevent this problem, you can minimize it by simply taking note of where your feathered neighbors habitually perch (trees, feeders, fences, power lines, etc.) and drying laundry as far from their hangouts as possible.

Be warned—in a growing number of communities, hanging laundry outside is either officially prohibited (as in some highly regulated neighborhoods) or simply frowned upon. If you live in the latter, you would be wise to take your neighbors' sightlines into account as you plan the best location for your laundry line. People take their views and vistas seriously, and one person's idea of wholesome housekeeping may be another's affront to all that is decent and civilized.

The level of civilization in your neighborhood may present yet another problem: thievery. City homeowners often learn the hard way that the criminal mind is not always a logical one. You would think that a backyard line full of humble shirts and sheets wouldn't be tempting. But sometimes the thrill of the caper exceeds the value of the loot. If your laundry line is visible from a public street or alley, keep an eye on it.

TECHNIQUE | PRIMING THE LINE

Before you use your outdoor line, take a damp rag or towel and wipe down the line to remove bird dirt and other grime that could leave a mark on your clean laundry. Be sure you're well equipped with plenty of clothespins and something to carry them conveniently, such as a basket that attaches to the line or a deep-pocketed apron.

ASIDE | AIR DRYING INDOORS

For laundry that won't tolerate the dryer and can't be hung outside, the best solution is a folding wooden laundry rack, available from hardware stores or various folksy mail-order catalogs. Set it up by an open window if there's a nice breeze, or on a screened-in porch. You won't get all the disinfectant benefits of sunlight that come from hanging laundry outside, but as long as everyone in your household is reasonably healthy and regularly showered, you won't need them. The extra weight of lingering moisture will cause knitted garments to stretch out of shape if hung to dry. Housewares stores sell inexpensive sweater dryers, which allow the garment to dry flat on a raised, mesh platform.

TECHNIQUE | PERFECTING PANTS WITHOUT IRONING

To give your cotton jeans and khakis a polished appearance, tumble them dry for 10 to 15 minutes. Remove them from the dryer. They will still be fairly damp. Fold them lengthwise as if you were going to hang them (either with a front crease or without). Throw a clean towel on the floor and put on a pair of clean socks. Hold the pants by the waistband so that the hems or cuffs touch the towel on the floor. Step on the hems and hold them in place with your foot while you tug on the waistband, gently smoothing and stretching the pants into shape. Step off the hems and finger press the crease, if desired. Apply a fragrant linen spray, if desired, and hang your pants upside down to dry overnight. In the morning, you'll have crisp, unwrinkled pants.

Clothespin techniques are equal parts art and science. The challenge is to clip each item to the line in such a way that it will look its best when dry (that's the art part) and make the most of the breeze without blowing away (that's the science). Although the particulars vary with the size and contours of your laundry, one technique applies to all: Be sure to fold about 1½ to 2 inches of fabric around the line before you place the clothespin to secure the laundry to the line.

Blouses and shirts Turn inside out to reduce fading. Hang by the hem, either buttoned (for optimal shape retention) or unbuttoned (for faster drying).

T-shirts Fold over line at underarm; pin just below the armhole.

Dresses Turn inside out to minimize fading. Pin at the shoulders or fold over line at underarm and pin just below the armholes.

Pants, shorts, skirts, and briefs Hang by the waistband with the front of the garment facing the direction of the wind; position pins along the back of the band, just behind the side seams.

Clothespin techniques are also family heirlooms. Pinning sheets to the line just like your mother taught you is a great way to honor your personal, emotional connections to tradition, family, and home. Use the suggestions below to supplement, not replace, the know-how you've inherited.

Pillowcases   Pin at the open edge, just inside the side seams, creating a breeze-catching opening on the windward side.

Sheets   Fold in half lengthwise. Pin one side of the open edge taut across the line. Bring the other edge up to the line, facing the wind. Pin the corners of the second edge an inch or two inside the corners of the first edge, creating a breeze-catching opening on the windward side.

Towels   Snap firmly a few times, to fluff up the flattened pile. Hang by the short edge.

4

PRIZED POSSESSIONS

1. BABY CLOTHES

2. FINE LINENS

3. NATURAL FIBERS

How to take pride and pleasure in caring for layettes, heirlooms, and other textile treasures.

IT'S A PLEASURE TO LAVISH A LITTLE EXTRA CARE ON THE most treasured textiles in your home. A soft cotton receiving blanket, knitted by a loving grandmother, keeps a newborn warm and safe all the way home from the hospital. A beautiful damask tablecloth, gleaming under candlelight, makes your family and guests feel special and cherished. A crisply ironed, faintly fragrant linen pillowcase feels deliciously cool and soft against your skin on a warm, summer night. A delicate, lace-edged handkerchief is a comforting companion for decades of weddings, anniversaries, christenings, and graduations.

1. BABY CLOTHES

If you are doing baby laundry, you are probably suffering from severe sleep deprivation, so this section will be short and simple. Babies are cuter than the rest of us, which is fortunate, because they're also considerably leakier than the rest of us. Babies are also considerably more sensitive than the rest of us, so baby laundry must be washed with a detergent that rinses away without leaving any irritating residues.

Because their clothing and linens are subjected to more protein stains (emanating from both ends) than typical laundry, stain removal is an unavoidable part of baby laundry. Following is a short list of common baby stains and their remedies.

TECHNIQUE | REMEDIES FOR BABY STAINS

BREAST MILK OR FORMULA *(original and regurgitated)*	Rinse well in cold water.
	For white fabrics, apply lemon juice and bleach in the sun.
	For colors, apply a paste of meat tenderizer and water thirty minutes before washing.
FOODS *(original and regurgitated)*	For fruits and vegetables, wet fabric and sprinkle with salt. Then rinse and pretreat with laundry detergent.
	For protein foods, use techniques for milk and formula as above.
FECAL MATTER	Remove as much loose soil as possible. Presoak in a solution of two tablespoons borax dissolved in one gallon of the hottest water fabric will tolerate for sixty minutes before laundering.

LAUNDERING DIAPERS

Cloth diapers are a healthy choice for babies and responsible choice for the environment. Parents who launder diapers at home, rather than hiring a service, appreciate knowing exactly what kinds of detergents and laundry additives are used.

Diapers require their own specially segregated wash loads and their own laundering process.

1. Shake soiled diapers over the toilet to remove anything that will succumb to gravity. Rinse away any remaining heavy soil.

2. Use a diaper pail with an airtight lid. Presoaking diapers with borax or bleach is optional and may cause the fabric to wear out faster.

3. Load diapers into the washer and run a soak cycle with hot water and detergent. When the soak cycle finishes spinning, run a regular, hot wash cycle with detergent and bleach or borax, if desired.

4. Diaper loads should go through two to three rinse cycles to remove all traces of detergent and laundry additives.

5. Add a half cup of white vinegar in the final rinse to soften and help clear away any remaining detergent residue. Never use fabric softener on diapers—it makes them less absorbent.

6. Line dry diapers in full sunlight or tumble dry on high heat.

2. FINE LINENS

Hundreds of years ago, linens were among a family's most treasured possessions. These luxuries were the result of arduous work in the fields and farms, followed by consummate skill at the spinning wheels and looms. A young girl would assemble her trousseau years before she'd start collecting admirers, embellishing select pieces by hand with delicately embroidered initials or spidery crocheted lace.

Today we tend to love these treasures from afar. Far too often, the finest works of textile artistry are locked away in attics and cupboards, only to see the light of day when company comes to dinner during the holidays. If you are fortunate enough to own fine linens, do your linens— and yourself—a favor and use them often. Long-term storage causes these fine fabrics to yellow and weaken at the folds. Making them a part of your daily life connects you to the people and pageantry of your past.

Caring for such keepsakes is a patient pleasure. It's immensely satisfying to restore linens to a snowy, pristine, fragrant state. And it's often not as finicky a process as you might think. After all, old-fashioned laundering was far more vigorous than today's methods. Your washer-dryer regimen is a veritable spa compared to the rigors of the washboard and lye soap.

Of course there is an element of risk in caring for anything that doesn't come with a contemporary care label. But linens can surprise you with their strength.

Cotton damasks   Vintage tablecloths, napkins, and bedding can be laundered in hot water and gentle detergent. Use the delicate cycle. Never use chlorine bleach; it will weaken the fibers and minimize the subtle contrasts of the damask design. Line dry until just damp, then iron promptly. If items are to be stored long term, dry completely and do not iron.

Sturdy linens, without lace or embroidery   If shrinking is not a concern, launder in hot water and gentle detergent on the gentle cycle. To minimize shrinkage, wash in cool water. Line dry until just damp, then iron promptly. If items are to be stored for a long time, dry completely and do not iron.

Linen may be machine dried on a short, low heat cycle. This results in a soft, gently rumpled appearance. However, tumble drying hastens wear and tear on the fibers, so it isn't recommended for heirlooms that you're planning to hand down to future generations.

Delicate and embellished linens   Hand wash in cool water with gentle detergent. After rinsing, roll item in a clean towel and press gently to remove excess water. Do not wring or twist. Line dry until just damp, then iron promptly. To iron an embroidered item without crushing it, place it right-side down on a soft towel and press gently on the wrong side.

3. NATURAL FIBERS

Even though synthetic fabrics have improved greatly in recent years, there's simply no substitute for quality natural fibers. Their appeal is part aesthetic, part historic. For centuries, we have cooled ourselves in breezy cottons, warmed ourselves in snuggly wools, and cosseted ourselves with the caress of silk. Fashions may change, but the fabrics of our ancestors remain our favorites.

Cashmere Cashmere is combed from the downy undercoat of Kashmir goats, which are raised in the high plateaus of China, Mongolia, and Tibet. The rugged climate of their homeland produces a fiber of incredible warmth and softness. Cashmere yarns can be finely spun for feather-light garments or thickly spun for soft, lofty sweaters. Cashmere's lightweight, breathable warmth keeps you comfortable almost year-round, on all but the stickiest summer days. For people who prickle at the touch of wool, cashmere is a cushy comfort when the weather turns cold.

Price is a reliable indicator of quality; bargain cashmere will shed, pill, and lose its shape more quickly. Trust your fingertips when shopping for cashmere; quality goods are softer and thicker to the touch. Cashmere lacks wool's springy resilience; the two fibers are often paired together in blends.

Although woven cashmere fabrics should always be dry-cleaned, most quality cashmere knits can be hand washed in cool water with mild soap. Rinse thoroughly; roll in a clean towel and squeeze gently to remove excess water. Never wring or twist. Gently coax the garment back to its original dimensions and dry flat.

Cotton This versatile fiber comes in countless guises, from crisp sheets to soft towels, from cuddly flannels to stretchy knits, from diapers to dress shirts. No other fiber is used in more ways than the fluff that surrounds the seeds of an unassuming tropical shrub.

Cotton was the cloth of ancient Egypt and India. Today China, India, and the United States produce most of the world's cotton. The best breeds of cotton grow the longest staples, or fibers; when spun, these fibers make the finest, strongest, smoothest yarns. Egyptian cotton and homegrown Pima and Sea Island cottons set the quality standards. These premium cottons are comparatively rare and are often blended with lesser varieties—a careful reading of the fiber content label will tell you whether your "Pima" sheets are truly 100 percent Pima.

Caring for cotton varies tremendously, depending on whether the item is knit or woven, loosely or tightly constructed. Nontreated cottons will shrink at first in a hot wash or dryer cycle; new garments and linens are sized to compensate for this. Woven cottons respond well to line drying, and yellowed whites often can be bleached in the sun without resorting to laundry additives. Knits that can't be tumble dried need special care. Because cotton is so absorbent, the weight of a wet garment can easily stretch it out of shape. Always handle wet knits gently and dry them flat.

Linen Long before trade routes brought Indian cottons to the cities of Europe, Europeans dressed themselves and their homes in linen. The pretty blue and white flowers of the flax plant bloom in midsummer, wherever the climate is temperate and the soil is moist. But the real beauty of flax is hidden in its stems, which are soaked, beaten, scraped, and spun to produce fibers fit for delicate finery, sturdy grain sacks, and everything in between.

This time-consuming, labor-intensive process explains linen's high price and relative scarcity. Ireland and Belgium are the world's foremost producers.

Linen is cooler than cotton because it's more absorbent and allows moisture to evaporate more quickly. These advantages make linen a favorite choice for summery shirts and sheets. In crisply tailored garments, however, pure linen wrinkles readily.

Most washable linens respond well to laundering in good detergent and hot water, as described in "Fine Linens," pages 60–61. Line drying in the sun keeps whites at their brightest.

Silk According to legend, silk was discovered almost 5,000 years ago when a silkworm cocoon fell from a mulberry branch into the bathtub of a Chinese empress. The warmth of the water caused the filaments of the cocoon to unravel. Regardless of its veracity, it's an enchanting story for an enchanting fiber. Silk is coveted the world over.

No other natural fiber provides such excellent insulation for warmth without weight. Silk absorbs dyes beautifully, resulting in colors of unrivaled richness. The colors of silk are made even more radiant by smooth fibers that reflect light to create a natural luster that shines through no matter how the silk is loomed.

Silk is as versatile as it is beautiful. The world's glossiest taffetas and richest velvets are made from it. Knitted silks range from lingerie-light refinement to chunky, raw handspuns. It sheds wrinkles with a minimum of fuss and springs back to shape when stretched. In terms of tensile strength, silk is tougher than cotton. But silk requires tender care to retain its luminous qualities.

Silks that have been specially treated to be washable require lukewarm water, non-alkaline soap, and minimal soaking. Handle them gently—silk fibers are weakened when wet. Never use chlorine bleach. Rinse thoroughly. A splash of white vinegar in the rinse water will help remove every trace of soap. Blot with a clean towel to remove excess water without wringing and line dry away from direct sunlight.

Many silks are to be dry-cleaned only. Check your care labels carefully.

Wool Breathable, absorbent, and soft, wool has been keeping us cozy for centuries. Spun from the renewable fleece of domesticated sheep, wool is woven and knitted into garments ranging from impeccable boardroom tailoring to slouchy Saturday styles. Wool resists wrinkles, static, perspiration odors, and even light rain showers. And it has an excellent memory—all most garments need to snap back to their proper shape and size is a good half hour of hanging out in a steamy bathroom.

Inexpensive grades of wool have given all wool an undeserved reputation for scratchiness. The finest wools, like lamb's wool and merino, are lofty and soft against the skin. Wool is produced around the world but much of the best comes from Australia, Great Britain, and the United States.

Lightweight wool woven fabrics make ideal summer suiting. And a finely loomed wool blanket is perfect for cool summer nights. But heavier wools spend the summer in storage, preferably scented by lavender sachets and cedar, waiting for the first frost of autumn.

For all its strength and sturdiness, wool should be laundered with care. Most woven wools are dry-clean only. Washable wools should be hand laundered in cool water with a non-alkaline soap. Rinse well and squeeze without wringing to remove as much water as possible. Dry flat.

Knitters have long been leery of washing by machine—the agitation, even in the gentle cycle, will cause wool knits to pill and felt. Felting occurs when friction causes wool fibers to lock together, thickening and shrinking the fabric—a desirable result if you're trying to fashion a beret but a disaster if you just want a cleaner ski sweater. Once wool is felted, it can't be undone. Machine-washable and dryable wools are specially treated with a chemical coating to prevent the fibers from felting.

Dry cleaning isn't really *dry*. The word dry in this case simply means that no water is used. Dry cleaning uses liquid solvents and detergents to remove dirt and odors from fabrics that can't tolerate water. Items are dried at low temperatures, then steamed and pressed.

Proper drying and steaming removes most of the chemical odors from dry-cleaned fabrics. Any remaining fumes, however, are trapped by the plastic bags cleaners use to wrap your clothes. As soon as you bring your dry cleaning home, remove the bags and hang the items in an airy place—an enclosed porch is ideal but any well-ventilated place will do. Leave them to air for at least an hour or two before putting them away.

Long-term storage in plastic bags has been known to do some strange things to fabrics. To prevent phantom staining and yellowing, cover seldom-used items with clean, old sheets to keep dust away. Invest in canvas hanging bags for expensive formal wear and heirloom table linens.

In response to the environmental concerns of their customers, more and more dry cleaners are offering new "green" methods and solvents that are kinder to people and the planet. Ask the cleaners you patronize about their practices and policies; and let them know you care about environmentally safer cleaning.

5

FINISHING TOUCHES

1. IRONING

2. FOLDING & ORGANIZING

3. STORING

How to press for success, fold, and put things
away—for the day or season.

It has long been an axiom of mine that the little things are infinitely the most important.
— SIR ARTHUR CONAN DOYLE

SMALL GESTURES MAKE A BIG IMPACT. IT TAKES ALL OF
a minute to line a drawer with scented paper. It takes no more than five minutes to
press a pillowcase. In these tiny slivers of time, between phone calls or before bed,
you make your home a haven.

If bringing out the ironing board is a rare event in your house, enhance your sense
of occasion with just the right music. If you're bored with the selection in your music
collection, sample something a little different from the following suggestions.

Come Away with Me, Norah Jones

Dinah Washington Sings Bessie Smith, Dinah Washington

The Essential Nina Simone, Nina Simone

Finally, Betty Carter

Look of Love, Diana Krall

Sunday at the Village Vanguard, Bill Evans Trio

1. IRONING

Ironing is a bit like cooking: You can certainly live without doing it but you occasionally suspect that the time you save isn't worth what you sacrifice.

What you give up is this: a small, but indelible, act of grace. It's the difference between penning a handwritten note and sending an e-mail.

The fact that ironing is no longer necessary in an age of one-hour shirts and (supposedly) wrinkle-free synthetics is the very thing that elevates it into a ritual. Ironing is a gift, an offering to yourself and the people you love. Iron a shirt for your sweetheart the night before an important presentation. Spread a pressed heirloom tablecloth to turn ordinary weeknight fare into a special birthday celebration. Press a lacy linen handkerchief for a bride-to-be (then tie it with a ribbon and tuck a tube of waterproof mascara into the bow).

But the benefits of ironing aren't only for special occasions. Ironing casual clothes that you normally wear straight from the dryer can give you a pleasant boost of confidence. You'll feel more polished and poised. You might even find yourself standing up straighter.

Few tasks are as pleasant and productive as smoothing your beautiful things into a state of perfection. To spend an evening transforming a wicker basket brimming with newly laundered clothes and linens into a closet full of crisp shirts and a stack of smooth, snowy napkins can be something akin to Zen. It's a task suited to quiet contemplation—just you, your thoughts, and the small triumph of tidiness that each freshly ironed item represents.

IRONING EQUIPMENT AND SUPPLIES

You probably already have just about everything you need for a satisfying session of ironing, but here's a checklist anyway.

:: Good lighting

:: A sturdy ironing board with a padded, heatproof cover, adjusted to a comfortable working height

:: A good iron with a clean, scorch-free soleplate

:: A spray bottle of distilled water or scented ironing water

:: An airy place to hang items to cool before putting them in the closet

:: A sleeve board (optional) if you prefer shirtsleeves without creases

:: A press cloth (a clean, lint-free dish towel or muslin rag)

:: Lint brush or tape roller

Begin with your spray bottle. Moisten your cottons and linens lightly, as uniformly as you can. Then roll them up neatly and put them aside for at least fifteen minutes, allowing the water to permeate the fibers thoroughly. Ironing well-moistened cloth is easier than spraying or steaming dry cloth on the ironing board, and you'll achieve better results. A generation ago it was standard practice to wrap up moistened items and store them in the fridge overnight. Today the standard is whatever your time allows. But it's wise to refrigerate any items that will remain moistened for more than two or three hours to prevent mildew.

Next preheat your iron to the lowest setting you'll be using. For example, if your basket contains cotton, linen, and silk, start with the silk setting—it's far less trouble to wait for the iron to warm up to the next level you need than to risk scorching something delicate with an iron that needed more time to cool than you thought it would. Then start with your low-temperature items. Never move the iron in circles; this will stretch the fabric. Use a back-and-forth motion that corresponds with the grain of the material.

Use a press cloth to keep silks and wools from scorching and getting shiny. A press cloth is a lint-free fabric (a piece of old cotton sheet will do nicely) that goes between the fabric and the iron.

Keep your spray bottle handy for fabrics that get dry before all the wrinkles are out. Once you're finished, hang or fold the item and put it aside to cool.

After you're done with the items that require the lowest heat setting, adjust the temperature of the iron accordingly for the remaining items in your basket.

Here are some general guidelines for selecting the correct temperature for each fabric. Always check care labels for specific instructions.

TIP | FABRIC TEMPERATURES

SILK	Low heat, dry press cloth, press right-side down
SYNTHETICS	Low heat
WOOL	Low heat, damp press cloth, press right-side down
COTTON BLENDS	Medium heat
COTTON	High heat
LINEN	Highest heat

IRONING A TAILORED SHIRT

There's only one real rule about ironing shirts: If you are utterly certain that your way is the One True Way, then you're probably right. If you've never ironed a shirt before, start with our method, below. Once you're comfortable, feel free to improve on it.

1. Iron the thickest parts first: the collar, the cuffs, and the buttonhole placket. Use plenty of steam.

2. Press the back yoke (the double thickness of fabric across the shoulders).

3. Press the sleeves. A) To press flat with a shoulder crease, lay the sleeve on the board so that the back of the shirt is facing up. Fold the sleeve lengthwise so that its lower edge lines up with the seam that runs from the underarm to the cuff. Then smooth the fabric

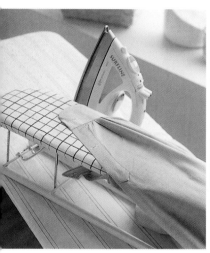

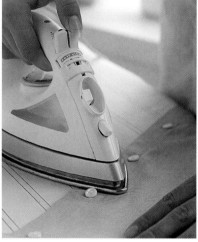

until both layers are flat. Press the
back of the sleeve. Flip it over.
Squirt any ironed-in wrinkles with
your spray bottle. Press the front.
B) To press without a crease,
insert a sleeve board into the
sleeve and press, shifting the fabric
until the whole sleeve is smooth.

4. Press the back of the shirt, then
press the button side of the front,
easing your iron around the buttons,
not over them.

5. Press the remaining side of the
front. Hang and button the top
collar button.

Ironing sheets and pillowcases will seem like utter lunacy to almost anyone who doesn't have servants. But it's worth doing at least once just to have the experience of sliding into a freshly pressed, exquisitely smooth, gently scented bed. It's like being in the embrace of a really, really good hotel.

It takes no more than twenty minutes to iron a top sheet, bottom sheet, and a few pillowcases. Try it some time when you'd otherwise spend that twenty minutes doing something regrettable—something involving a pint of ice cream, perhaps. Then tuck yourself in for the night. If you don't wake up in the morning feeling completely serene, like well-rested royalty, you don't have to do it again.

TECHNIQUE | HOW TO CLEAN YOUR IRON

To remove melted plastic or starch buildup from the soleplate, open up a paper grocery bag and spread it on your ironing board, printed-side down. Sprinkle generously with table salt. Heat the iron to medium-high and iron over the salt until the gunk adheres to the salt. Use an old, thick towel to rub any remaining salt from the iron.

To remove rust stains from your iron, apply a dab of petroleum jelly to the stains and rub with a soft cloth. Follow with a clean cloth moistened with isopropyl alcohol to remove all traces of petroleum jelly.

2. FOLDING & ORGANIZING

If being organized were truly easy, there would be no piles. There would be no towers of towels sliding into stacks of junk mail. There would be no getting dressed in the laundry room because all the clean clothes are sitting, semifolded, on top of the dryer. There would be no socks on the dining room table. There are two tricks to organizing your freshly laundered clothes and linens:

:: Rethink what your mother taught you about folding.

:: Create easy-to-reach, pleasantly scented storage places.

If you really, truly love to fold laundry—if it makes you proud and happy to see the results of your laundering labors stacked up like soldiers, indexed by color, and arranged chronologically by purchase date—then the following advice is not for you. If you are an ordinary, time-starved mortal, fretfully disorganized and almost always a little behind schedule, then read on.

It is a myth that there is only one right way to fold laundry. Life is far too short to worry about whether the creases in your top sheet are symmetrical. This is not to say that folding is optional—few of us want to look as though our daily clothes and linens were chosen from a heap on the bedroom floor, unless we are teenagers who are pointedly disregarding the constraints of bourgeois values. But folding is a flexible discipline that can be modified as much as you wish.

Have you ever stepped into someone else's powder room and thought less of them because their hand towels weren't folded the right way? Of course not. So why not apply the same tolerant standards to yourself?

FOLDING LINENS

For linens, the rule is this: Do the absolute minimum of whatever you need to do to fit them into your linen closet with a minimum of wrinkles. Folding is not recommended for seldom-used heirloom linens. Long-term folds can weaken and break down fibers. Instead roll them around mailing tubes and wrap them in old sheets. Fitted sheets can be tricky. Here are two methods to try.

TECHNIQUE 1: LARGER SPACES

 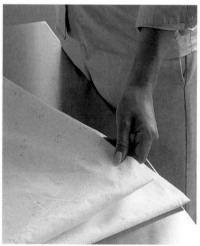 

1. Spread the sheet, gathered-side up, on a clean, flat surface. Smooth all four sides evenly.

2. Fold crosswise, bringing top to bottom, so that all gathered sides are folded to the inside, forming an even rectangle with rounded corners.

3. Then fold as needed to fit into your closet or drawer.

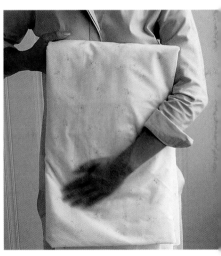

1. Pick two adjacent corners and tuck one into another.

2. Repeat with remaining corners. Bring all four corners together, tucking the second two into the first two.

3. Smooth the gathered top and fold the sides in evenly. Then continue to fold as needed.

FOLDING CLOTHING

For clothing, do the absolute minimum of whatever you need to do to wear them without embarrassment. Just because your mom taught you to fold your sweaters in quarters—or sixths—doesn't mean it's the only way at your disposal.

Better still, hang everything your closets will accommodate.

Casual pants and jeans   Hang by the cuff, and the weight of the waistband and pockets will help to smooth out lap creases and knee wrinkles.

Sweaters   One of the cardinal rules of clothing care has always been Never Hang Sweaters. But walk into any good department store and you will find sweaters on hangers by the hundreds. At home, however, not any old hanger will do. Padded hangers are the best choice for sweaters. Wooden hangers with gently contoured shoulders are an acceptable alternative. Short, lightweight sweaters are the best candidates for hanging. Long, heavy sweaters should never be hung. If in doubt, put the sweater on a hanger and look at the shoulders carefully; if they show the slightest bit of stretch, it's not a candidate for the closet.

Tablecloths   Fold in quarters lengthwise, then drape over a trouser hanger with a nonslip, rounded crossbar.

3. STORING

Most storage problems are either quantity problems or quality problems. Quantity problems occur when you have more stuff than space. Quality problems occur when you have adequate space but you don't use it effectively.

Strategies for insufficient storage Before you try to fix your storage shortage by hiring a contractor to build an extra wing, take a long, merciless look at your possessions. Are you still hanging onto queen-size sheets, even though you traded up to a king-size mattress two years ago? Give them away—to thrift shops, to friends with summer cottages, to anyone who will be glad to take them out of your way. The same policy goes for clothing: If you've gone one year without wearing it, you're not going to miss it. Send it packing.

It's often helpful to segregate long-term storage from everyday use items. You can create a surprising amount of closet space just by putting your out-of-season things elsewhere. Invest in some good, insect proof chests or storage bags. Some are narrow enough to slide under a bed. Others can be stashed high on a closet shelf or up in the attic.

Be sure to wash or dry-clean everything before putting it into storage—moths are attracted to dirt, oils, perspiration, and food stains. Natural alternatives to smelly mothballs include commonly available ingredients such as cedar, eucalyptus, lavender, pennyroyal, rosemary, thyme, tobacco, and white pepper. You can find most of these at your local natural foods store. Less commonly known are powdered orris root (from a type of lily) and pyrethrum (made from the dried flowers of an African chrysanthemum).

If you're still short of space after you've sifted through the things you no longer use and stashed your out-of-season items, call in an expert. Closet organizing specialists will measure your closets, count your hangers, and design a configuration of shelves, rods, and baskets to help make the most of your available space. Building supply stores stock how-to books and materials for do-it-yourselfers. Two people can easily redo a closet in a weekend.

CREATING QUALITY STORAGE

If there's a huge pile on top of your dresser but the drawers are empty, you're not alone. If you have space you're not using, the solution is simple: Just give yourself an incentive to take that last little step.

Fragrance works beautifully in this regard. Line your drawers with beautifully scented paper. Clip aromatic clothespins onto the hangers in your closet. Tuck some fragrant soaps into an armoire. Every time you open a closet or a drawer, you'll get a breath of freshly scented air. And the trace of scent that lingers on your clothes and linens will reward your extra effort.

REORGANIZING YOUR STATE OF MIND

Perhaps the most important aspect of organizing is making peace with the piles. Taking pleasure in home keeping is very different from trying to measure up to an unsustainable standard of perfection. The pristine pictures of homes featured in magazines and books, even this one, represent hours of work by photographers and stylists. Once the cameras are gone, life in these homes returns to normal. People spill things. The resident white cat sheds on the black velvet upholstery. And the laundry occasionally goes undone.

When your schedule fills up, it's perfectly all right to let nonessential tasks slide. When your obligations subside, you'll find time to restore order again. Caring for laundry is one of life's constants. So is caring for yourself.